Dear Parent:
Your child's love of reading starts here!

Every child learns to read in a different way and at his or her own speed. Some go back and forth between reading levels and read favorite books again and again. Others read through each level in order. You can help your young reader improve and become more confident by encouraging his or her own interests and abilities. From books your child reads with you to the first books he or she reads alone, there are I Can Read Books for every stage of reading:

SHARED READING
Basic language, word repetition, and whimsical illustrations, ideal for sharing with your emergent reader

BEGINNING READING
Short sentences, familiar words, and simple concepts for children eager to read on their own

READING WITH HELP
Engaging stories, longer sentences, and language play for developing readers

READING ALONE
Complex plots, challenging vocabulary, and high-interest topics for the independent reader

ADVANCED READING
Short paragraphs, chapters, and exciting themes for the perfect bridge to chapter books

I Can Read Books have introduced children to the joy of reading since 1957. Featuring award-winning authors and illustrators and a fabulous cast of beloved characters, I Can Read Books set the standard for beginning readers.

A lifetime of discovery begins with the magical words "I Can Read!"

Visit www.icanread.com for information on enriching your child's reading experience.

Pinkalicious®
Fashion Fun

To Ellen
—V.K.

The author gratefully acknowledges
the artistic and editorial contributions of
Daniel Griffo and Kamilla Benko.

I Can Read Book® is a trademark of HarperCollins Publishers.

Pinkalicious: Fashion Fun
Copyright © 2016 by Victoria Kann

PINKALICIOUS and all related logos and characters are trademarks of Victoria Kann. Used with permission.

Based on the HarperCollins book *Pinkalicious* written by
Victoria Kann and Elizabeth Kann, illustrated by Victoria Kann
All rights reserved. Manufactured in the U. S. A.
No part of this book may be used or reproduced in any manner whatsoever without
written permission except in the case of brief quotations embodied in critical articles and reviews.
For information address HarperCollins Children's Books, a division of HarperCollins Publishers,
195 Broadway, New York, NY 10007.
www.icanread.com

Library of Congress Control Number: 2015958413

ISBN 978-0-06-241077-1 (trade bdg.) — ISBN 978-0-06-241076-4 (pbk.)

16 17 18 19 20 LSCC 10 9 8 7 6 5 4
❖
First Edition

Pinkalicious®
Fashion Fun

by Victoria Kann

HARPER
An Imprint of HarperCollinsPublishers

Rose and Molly came over to play.

Molly was holding

a mysterious folder.

"What is in there?" I asked.

"They're pictures
of designer clothing
and fashion shows that I've collected
from magazines," Molly explained.

"Those are beautiful outfits!" Rose said.

"I want dresses like that," I said.

"Mommy has a dress
like the one in that picture.
Let's look in her closet," I said.
"We can have our own
fashion show!"

Just then, Mommy came in.

"What are you doing?" Mommy asked.

"My clothes are not for playtime!"

"We're fashion designers," I said.
"Please use your imaginations,
not my clothing," said Mommy.

"Ew, imaginary clothes!"
said Rose.
"Please play in your room,
not my closet!" said Mommy.

We looked at the pictures again.

"I like those shoes

with bows," I said.

"The bows look like pasta,"
said Molly.

"I have an idea!" I said.

"We need glue!" I said.

"Let's get twist ties!" said Rose.

"Don't forget glitter!" said Molly.

"What are you doing?" asked Peter.

"Can I do it, too?"

I thought about it.

"You can be a photographer," I said.

"Yes!" he yelled.

"Say cupcake and smile!"

The doorbell rang.

My friends' mothers

were here to pick them up.

"Have a seat," said Mommy.

"The girls have a surprise for you."

"Are you ready?" I asked my friends.

"It's showtime!"

"Welcome to our fashion show!"
Rose said as we paraded
into the living room.

"We used things
around the house
to make our clothes,"
I added.

"Look at my newspaper
and coffee-filter pants!"
said Molly.

"The flowers on my vest
are cupcake liners," said Rose.

"My dress is made
from Bubble Wrap!" I said.
Click! went Peter's camera.

"Bravo!" Rose's mommy cheered.

"Show off your outfits and twirl!"

We twirled faster and faster!

Paper, ribbons,

and cupcake liners went flying!

Peter got closer and closer,

trying to get the perfect picture. . . .

POP, POP, POP, POP!

My dress was ruined!

I almost started to cry,

but then I heard clapping!

"Marvelous!" Molly's mommy said.
"You made a dress
that can be worn two different ways,
and now we can see your
sparkly macaroni shoes!

"If you stick with it," she said,
"you'll have a career in fashion!
I love how you used food
 in your designs."
"Oh yes!" I said. I was inspired.

I smiled and grabbed my sketchbook.

I had an idea:

a cupcake dress!

I wonder if I could use real frosting.